Born in Sydney in 1952, Robyn Rowland grew up in the New South Wales seaside town of Shellharbour. She lived in New Zealand from 1978 to 1980, and in England in 1984; she has visited Ireland regularly since 1983. Her first book of poetry, *Filigree in Blood*, was published by Longman Cheshire in 1982, and her poems have been widely published in Australian journals and magazines. Dr Robyn Rowland is well known publicly for her work in bringing social and feminist issues into the public debate on the new reproductive technologies. Her most recent book is *Living Laboratories: Women and Reproductive Technologies*.

PERVERSE
Serenity

Robyn Rowland

SPINIFEX

Spinifex Press Pty Ltd
504 Queensberry Street
North Melbourne Vic. 3051
Australia

First published by William Heinemann Australia
Published in 1992 by Spinifex Press

Edited by Jill Taylor
Designed by R. T. J. Klinkhamer
First edition typeset by Bookset
Changes to second edition typeset by Claire Warren
Made and printed in Australia by The Book Printer

CIP

   Rowland, Robyn, 1952– .
    Perverse serenity.

   ISBN 1 875559 13 2

   I. Title.

A821.3

... And what you thought you came for
Is only a shell, a husk of meaning
From which purpose breaks only when it is fulfilled
If at all. Either you had no purpose
Or the purpose is beyond the end you figured
And is altered in fulfilment ...

T. S. Eliot Little Gidding

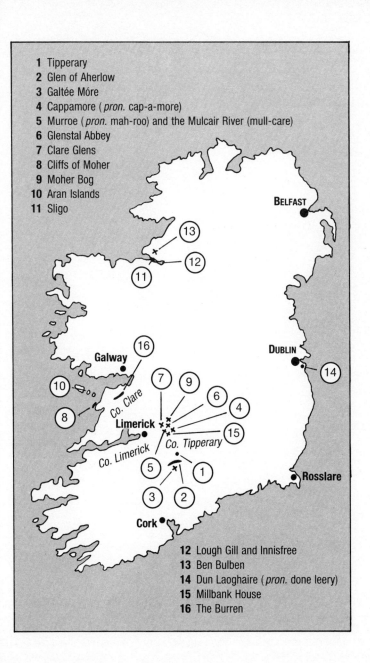

1 Tipperary
2 Glen of Aherlow
3 Galtée Móre
4 Cappamore (*pron.* cap-a-more)
5 Murroe (*pron.* mah-roo) and the Mulcair River (mull-care)
6 Glenstal Abbey
7 Clare Glens
8 Cliffs of Moher
9 Moher Bog
10 Aran Islands
11 Sligo

12 Lough Gill and Innisfree
13 Ben Bulben
14 Dun Laoghaire (*pron.* done leery)
15 Millbank House
16 The Burren

BELFAST

DUBLIN

Galway

Co. Clare

Limerick

Co. Limerick

Co. Tipperary

Rosslare

Cork

ACKNOWLEDGEMENTS

Poems from *Perverse Serenity* have been published in the *Age*, *Quadrant*, *Overland*, *Westerly*, and *Luna*. 'The Storm' appears in the anthology *Moments of Desire* edited by Susan Hawthorne and Jenny Pausacker (Penguin, 1989).

The epigraph to 'The Storm' is from Jeanette Winterson's novel *The Passion* (Bloomsbury, 1987), page 146.

CONTENTS

PART ONE

Searching   2
The beginning   4

PART TWO

Juggling   10
End in view   12
The risk   14
Re-leaving   16
Airborne   18

PART THREE

Wavering   20
Wasting   22
Uphill, still climbing   24
Toward clarity   27
Perverse serenity   29

PART FOUR

Finale	32
When love goes	34
Losing you	36
Changing	38
After Carringbush Ceili	40
Surviving single	43
Offerings	45
Reassessing	47
Dolphins	49
if	50
Black spring	51
Murroe	55
Ahead	56
Recurrent tug	57

PART FIVE

Winter surfaces	60
The final season	62
Spent	64
The storm	68
To satisfy	70
Glossary	73

PART ONE

SEARCHING

Dislocated to find location I come in search of family,
traces followed with perverse avidity by those whose
stories in their stolen land take short breath; counting
the stars for all the Irish exiled by famine, pain, or
that great roving spark burning in their bloodline still.
Cappamore's Virgin centring the town would be enough.
Gazed upon mercilessly by her unflickering mother's scorn,
harrassed by the toll of the priest's word and chafed by
the bleats of neighbours sure in numbers, prods in alien
pews remained only on sufferance. I see their exit written
like a psalm, accompanied by the weeping organ, full of the
ragged beauty of poems. And they grieved for the place,
pagan as it is; hills stabbed by crosses, crevices breeding
groves to the virgin. I place my hand on the grey rock of
an old barn, older than I have understanding for,
watching the turf cut. Long before, long after my shadow
has tossed itself in and out of life, the chunks will be
stacked and dried waiting for its slow burn of winter.
Nearby, Kathleen O'Neill spends each evening in this front
room, dark wood carved into the bar, roof thatched
against night, flags softened by old squares of carpet,
their pile trod soft. Two hundred and fifty years old
this room; older than my white country.
Clocks tick loud without hurry in rhythm with the
talk; up and down between laughter and the
worn worries of country life. The old black cat sleeps on
assured of its place. Evenings here bring parts
of a jigsaw to a whole, a place, a good fit, and the
musty smell of peat brings comfort on cooler nights, and
I take my pint of guinness before bed. Rural Ireland rubs a

grain of memory. Green beyond belief, marked by age and suffering, I feel it part of some old stirring: the place, the voices familiar. Reverent and irreverent alike know it when the strings are played and the note is true. Fuschia, tree-tall, drops its crimson purple flowers in tears onto the road.

Ireland
July 1983
A

THE BEGINNING

1.
There I entered Ireland —
down the long drive, circuitous
curled snug under colossus rhododendrons;
through that track by the farm
stinging nettles poised on each side;
past the lonely bull
torn from his heifers
shouldering each other
twitchy in the glens.

There were you by the hives —
that bee-loud stillness —
where all the sweetness of Glenstal is found.
You had tossed aside your Tunisian keeper's hat
reaching for the queen quite unafraid —
your fear waits in another glade.
And there was peace
beside the lake
green corners of it tranquil
green enough to subdue
even your bidden restlessness.

2.
But up here
away from Limerick's lights
that stud the valley deepening below,
turf on Moher Bog is
softly jagged in twilight;

bog cotton whimpers white
brushing the dark peat;
that one star is planted into pale evening
calling in blackness
the taunting glow of night-sky
to shadow us.
Disquiet trembles in the coiling breeze:
'why are you here'?

Our talk twists and turns
like paths round the Abbey
always leading to the same beginning:
how the heart can quickly love,
how thought can spring so deftly to accord,
and hurt drive piston fast
to strengthening doubt.
Your agitation frets, disturbs.
Uncertain for the first time
I stir silently, begin to query all,
even that intimacy I breathe by:
to shine in the corners of the other's mind
to keep close in the twining tendrils of daily love
its wash and drain
in which the pace of my life
is measured, safe.

Must those threads flex and sometimes break
or like elastic bands entwining a wrist,
embed, curb circulation,

print tattoo patterns, disfiguring skin?
Perhaps your 'empty peace' is best,
calm care of the loving many, the loose tugging
when you stray too far
or night becomes dawn before returning

and who would not hesitate to name
what love is

3.
Beginning eager, fervent
firework-high
you blaze Roman Candle bright
against my cheek
while I hold, suspicious, static
to the solid myth of my life
trust in it unbroken,
weighing this seeming flare
against my steady lights of home.
Tested, scalded and feverous
I hold fast.
Against this your desire gutters.

Here I fail.
    Fail
to know the human heart well enough
that it can be faithful, betray, and still love;
to learn that moments are all we have, soft and sturdy,

between their erratic tick
slips the hook, the shadow;
to understand that there is no fidelity in flesh
tempted often by love or passion
or a kind of childish greed
and even home love through the years
had found relief in half-light
from my beacon's constant beam.

I fail
to seize this moment.
Desire clots in me.

4.
Returned to my dry country
wearing its new coat of rain
like some foolish child in a garish mackintosh,
I choke for that old and softer light.
My mind strains to still caged restlessness,
draws on home love to vanquish yearning.
My hand reaches out to flick the switch.
I watch it relearn habits of the daily past
small knacks for crossing between two worlds
even as you lean back into the custom of thirteen years.

Drinking tea your hands fold firmly around the bowl;
your habit brushes the flags stone-cold;
routine, gentle but persistent, parcels up your day.

Both bound with raffia thread
into our divergent lives,
we only connect
knock each other in passing
accidental, surprised

and drifting solid but unreachable
the misted possible
as Innisfree in hazy morning shimmers.

PART TWO

Australia
July 1983
T

JUGGLING

I am learning to live
                         with the juggler
     red balls
          blue balls
               rosella pure
in mind's eye
                      momentary grip
struggling, me
                  to fit them
together, we want
     back into the clown's open moving mouth
                     constant in negative

Puppeteer's lines cut
                     puppet free-flailing
grapples for control

and falling I see two white horses
running wildly for all the world
as if they were free, fenced

Is this it? Beginning or middle
                   it comes too soon
     or too late
          fetus
             I tear the sack
force first limb

                              hand
waiting to stretch neck free
                              cold rush of air
to make warm familiar fluid
     ice-pain shock proving flesh not gone
                              not gangrenous
coming apart, I am. Peace, peace.

Australia
July 1983
T

END IN VIEW

Yours is the shock
         recoil after the blast
though I say little
         stunned to silence
in a riotous mind
         I grip hard to still.
Yours is the choice
         the route marked 'out'
somehow you do not take
         but stand holding the walls apart
protective while I cower
         frantic inside.
Yours is the clean grazed hope
         the sting of salty open skin
watching me stumble lost and dying
         inside myself.

We exhaust ourselves with talking, talking
         bodies ragged and thin
hare pelts stretched on the fence to dry
         bones knobbling, flesh falling.
Remembering — membering — membering
         past love, past places, past need.
Endlessly we chew and gnaw and lick
         some wound we cannot see
or find cause for, but want desperately
         to heal.

There was a wound once
        in your thigh. Sliver of wood
from a rotted fence pierced there
        but skin healed, wound closed
only to shoot its splinter
        months later from its fester
under the sealed flesh.
        Fresh clean scar.
Will we whiten in the sun
        when summer throws its warm blend
of light across our skin?

THE RISK

for Lynne

You visit seeking counsel, bringing tulips
because they seem 'right' for me,
their blaze of sturdy wholeness.
I hesitate before the red and yellow riot,
burlesque of joy opening to tarantula centres
black, furry, inner petals spiked.

Eyes touch. And you see no Delphic wisdom here,
both of us seeking some lost hungry self.

Wavering, in collusion, we balance old loves
flashing frieze of crystal
on sticks crazy clowns skilfully control
unicycles wobbling to inevitable collision
teetering between the unfamiliar and the known,
future passion and love past.
Only unchecked speed keeps us capering
legs judging the spin, spokes haywire
in lurch and zoom.
Recalling old fairytales of daring romance
willing them to be more than dusty relics
of childhood
we remake them over
yearning for one bright flare within the flames
before the ash.
Giddy on champagne and possibility
we back-pedal bang into adolescence
shatter the past to crystal rain.

'Go for it'.
Your flinging heart uncertain
head lost you landed sure.
Boneshaking love.

Now you wait
you tell me
for my 'Phoenix trick' —
as if there *were* a fire
as if the ashes *were* still warm
and the golden bird girds herself in readiness.
But there is no flame, no warmth here
just a steady downpour
torrent from impact, smashing its needle revenge.
Monsoon seasons of the heart thrash me.
I flounder, splintering.
Tulips shred, their blaze bee-gold and bloodied
slit over and again in reflection.
Dark legs scuttle between raindrop chips.

My past fragments.
Shards impale the heart.

Leaving Australia
August 1983
T

RE-LEAVING

Dry-eyed and terrified
I watch your dear face
your tears
melt into dawn.
And I am moving away
tunnelled in confusion
toward a hazy opening
and back
I'm going back
to find that lost wandering part
knocked from myself,
I must have stumbled.

I want.
I want so badly
and need to know its face
the shape of its features
focus on it
clear as the pure deepness
of Loch Gill's holy spring.

And if the frost and winter bite
of homecoming
is clenched tight between your lips
on returning
I will still have it
afterflare to burn in my mind
when past is too dark
and far away
to remember

I would
could
did
once
soar spontaneous
rosella free in
one great arch
so fast and high
I became a rainbow
curved across blankness
bright before dust.

In flight
August 1983

AIRBORNE

I read Lowell's tumult of poems on age.
Poinsettia-red they stab the page
like star-knives in the thunderous heart.
Does death come beckoned by fear?
Do we know pre-doomed the track
it takes winding its way slowly
or in quickstep toward us?
Like flying, how do we judge the pace?
I feel the rush toward its grip
like never before
feel the growling caress of its bestial breath
taste those lips tight on mine.
Stop . . . stop . . . there must be a way,
is this what it is . . .
the digging in of the heels
on the downward rush?

The tunnel lengthens.
Will there be rest?
Will the mind stop
heart cease, pain fade,
oil drain, watercolour to blank sheet?
Will there be sweet suffocating out of sky
by laurel and linden
by hedges of blood-fuschia tree-high?
Give me white calm
peace past remembering.

I cling to the disconnected intimacy
of sleep,
four hundred slumbering strangers share
the illusion of closeness.

PART THREE

Ireland
August 1983
A

WAVERING

We weary ourselves with
wandering country roads,
scattered stolen hours
driven into our lives.
Selfish for understanding
fused in reflection
we cannot stop
risk
face-to-face
close-eyed
breath-blending gaze.
This car a metal brace
runs us parallel in circles.
We go on.

Unsure what we share but this thin time
hurting each other with questions
that blur past certainties
wincing, smarting from the chafe and cut of words
we peel back our lives
raw and flinching.

At night, grappling with the onward push of day
you linger for the grazing brush of lips
wanted but not sought.
You will not now approach
keening your anguish silently.
I strain toward that soft hurt part of you
sealed tight
pollen set hard and brown in the comb

refusing to flow fluid on the tongue.
You want too much:
this closeness without touch.

My hands weeding today
clutched some unseen nettles.
Fingers swollen, stinging
I throb into the dark.

Ireland
August 1983
A

WASTING

Your body carries
the smooth bronze of this foolish summer —
no rain in Ireland.
You are sinew, strung muscle, blithe strength
a finer study of my father's limbs
arteries pulsing with exertion.
Nut-brown bloom is on you
and this mountain is no challenge
to your springing step,
though once the peak is attained
small crossing of its summit before descent.
Supple as the Mulcair over rocks
you move across terrain familiar as your hand
and the years tracking your eyes
beginning to furrow mortality.
Rapid urgency to move drives you
to expel, dispense
that bursting energy, danger in your flesh.

Decision made,
celibate, you fold your body away
like a best shirt
or those silk stockings my mother saved
in the war,
kept in a drawer till the battles ended
they were moth-riddled, mildewed from the damp.
I ache for this wasting,
to know age will melt you slowly to shapelessness
like old wax scraped from the frames
the honey long spun out.

Juiceless, left in the sun to soften
it will be reformed, reshaped,
no longer a container for that sweetness
but flareless candle,
life burned down inside,
wax melted inward
to lightless stub.

Ireland
August 1983
A

UPHILL, STILL CLIMBING

Into this Midas season
lumbers Galtée Móre
towering above the Glen of Aherlow.
It has flickered
through my sleep
since first you promised this climb,
always just out of reach
firefly in the dark of dreaming.
Now it strides belligerent
into solidity, steepness mocking.
I quiver with doubt.

This special day for you,
Feast of the Transfiguration,
began again the anguished battle
your voice white with struggle,
in that twisted place where
no joy, no mischief survives.
Why suffer it?

You walk ahead, bearded, rod in hand,
scene bearing filmy resemblance
to coloured pictures, Old Testament
biblical men leading their uncertain followers
toward dark wastes they call promised land.
Eyes never leaving your footfall
I am shepherded
with stories of your Mount Sinai climb,
the awe of standing where Moses
broke himself into god. I see it.

Thirsty we stop beside a spill of water.
Springs on this mountain are clear from Gaia's womb
tasting of earth and flesh;
moss, breast-soft, velvets the stones;
heather sprinkles its lilac hope
to pleasure the bees.

Steepening, steps smaller,
muscles tear into climbing
the final rocky face.
Hair-fine air withholds itself,
pulses thump
chest all lung and chambers.
Pleasure or penance?
The summit rounded like horizons never reached
falls to flatness.
Stunned I walk the roof of the world
all Ireland patched below.

I knew all along it would be here.
White blazing cross, Arthurian bold into the rock,
surely no mountain in Ireland
could sit
peaceful
without the stab of deity.
My rush of anger howls on implacable flint.
I watch you moving away inside
you think toward the inner spring;
wrestling to see that clear trickle
raindrop pure within the cleft of yourself

which followed upstream finds your god.
Sadness sags in me
clouds drop weighty
blocking the green below.

I rant, abandoned. I tell you
'We cannot engage a concept,
only connect with people,
their small joy, their foolishness,
their battered faces and bruised neediness;
with the real sweaty palms of them,
in their crazy reckless dance'.

Ireland
August 1983
A

TOWARD CLARITY

1.
You know what it's like:
intensity of night
entering the trees
before even sky succumbs;
a sea so perfect and deep
it scorns paint or celluloid;
shock fall of hair
blind with sunlight
swift heavy
scattering your vision to wheatfields
or the tossed softness of silk
in pollen-bright sun.
This love
fiery, solar-born
I expose to,
beg
for its scorch full on my face.

Quick like that
flash-bright like that
sweeping
            dazzling like that,
                        I ignite for you.

2.
But you shake gold flecks
from your sight
steady yourself from impact

one hand reaching behind
to find anchor in the cold rock,
draw breath
            in the shades of years'
            long-bred patience:
                        'It will pass.'

I came with summer in my eyes
the bare passion of hope,
saw chords
thrum their vibrancy in you
watch them tautening now
to measured meaningless words
you yourself admit
wash as so much driftwood
to a flameless fire.

Now you will endure
long nights, the dark as blank page,
sea's pale clawing at the grey beach,
that constant irritation of the eye
you rub but keep secretly
to remind you
once
you saw it burn,
firestorm
            inside the perilous calm of your days.

Ireland
August 1983
A

PERVERSE SERENITY

This cringing
        longing for peace,
                this *disease* of emptiness —
                        terminal peace

What antidote but anger
        pure and sweet as honey
                red rich as blood
                        broken on the rock

Smash this death
        false submission
                I am the life and the way
                        here is the living flame

Through love alone
                all things live

Love in her tattered cloak
        stumbling blinded weather-worn
                bludgeoned by robbers
                        hopeless with yearning for rest

bears more courage, more strength
        more radiance
                gives   gives   gives more
                        than this perverse serenity

PART FOUR

Australia
August 1983
T

FINALE

You think I forget
your odd slope of shoulder
downy furrow of chest,
bud-swell of buttock.
Or the smooth hairless touch of inner thigh,
the tender care of that delay
bred from a match of bodies
seeming more right
than even potters
could hand-mould.

I don't forget.
Minds with no god
bodies with no lover
are vast with remembering.

Nor do I forget
that calm core of terror,
the shape of your frenzied fist
afterimage in the dark.
And the smooth grip
of your tongue around words
denying   her   her   them
while our bed still carries
memories of betrayal.

What picture show
the mind can make,
like those flickering
obscene movie stands

in 'love' shops
where men slot in coins
watching
soured intimacy for sale
never sure which part
of put-up passion
they'll cash in on.

Pruned trees are abrupt.
I do not recognise this sky
left naked now and wondering.
Honeysuckle struggles
where I failed to wire it.
Daphne Odora begins flowering.
Across its first pure opening
overwhelming sweetness,
I wrench curtains
break music
bring the fierce fire of alcohol close.
Into five solitary days
I burn myself black.

Australia
August 1983
T

WHEN LOVE GOES

1.
In pain
I choose withdrawal
shrink backward into my lair
earthed in night's dark,
nothing to companion me, no-one —
just the black-feathered beat of wings
the scrabble of claws on tender sun-pink skin

ripping, ripping.

2.
I hear it first as from a long way off
trapped inside
spinning, closing fast,
this red-veined scream,
animal howl, woman's keening that rises, rises
stretched out streaming along my yearning.

It is carried silent
and passes into silence.

I am left licking, licking
where no wound is,
but the grazing echo.

3.
Each night I wake
to this silence
strong and lung-filled,
as when a spear shreds bone,
or a scream burns at the stake.

It is love dying,
slowly

in torment

writhing somewhere
in the attic of my soul
alone
dust-blown.

Australia
August 1983
T

LOSING YOU

One hungry step took me from you
stretching, tearing our siamese bonds
wrenching flesh from flesh
trunk from root, the mandrake screaming.

Here was the dance of reluctance,
yet I went, torn,
grafting myself into new growth.
If I said it were ordained
would you believe it
or would you say
some siren had gone ranting
lost in an ocean of youth's desires?

This is the colder time
we ceased to believe in
our guards dropping
in the surety of daily loving
and the real bond of it.

Memory carries the dew-grazed dawn of our love;
lost domains across which we strode and knew the paths;
up-weight of your hand under my elbow
when I stumbled;
it outlasts us, even our love —
if only our pain.

Ghosts gather in the room, familiar faces:
look here the unsure eyes of youth
fearful, anticipating rejection;

there strides the good-time ghost
features bold and smooth with laughter
aglow with knowing;
and in the corner, smile inward and secret
the sweet unnamed pleasures of our sharing.

If only it were all right
just to go on
along the path once taken,
to stop seeking sources
for that taunt of water far off
a trampled path falling from the wood;
be blinded to the blue-blade and red-black fringed
Ulysses butterfly flitting off
between the racket of bramble
and clustered thicket,
the great arch of oak and tangled moss.
If only it were all right
I would fall in with your measured pace
that we two once thought
stride enough for a pair well-matched,
the trail so clear and the exciting dark before us.

CHANGING

I stood uncertain among threads twisted at my feet
dropped haphazardly by the tangle of comfortable years.
Now I have plaited them fine and rough into this great rope,
peacock blues and greens in a thai-silk flash, at its finest,
broken-brown of waves at the Heads when the river floods,
                                            at its roughest.
But this knurled cable is so heavy to lift.
Many times I could willingly have dropped it,
so much easier had it been a pebble in the sling of the mind
to whizz fast and light leaving me still with breath.
But now with one driving lunge and
muscle pain beyond snapping strength
I cast my line headlong from these cliffs,
watch it snake and spiral mid-air
splaying wild like a fall of coloured arrows
to tug tight, tense,
in some unseen landing place.

This edge of land where I balance
falls sheer to vanish in a raven-black pitch of sea
rocked, spiked with waves, hungry for seabirds that
shriek in skids down its face
only to rise screaming into the gulf of air.
Precipitous and thrilling,
Cliffs of Moher in the inner selfscape.

But there is no feathered safety for me to cross this breach
only these two hands, scarred
rope-burned, fretting at the task
gripping, ungripping, clutching
one grasp at a time.

How it would help at least to *see* the other side
its features, cliff and crevice, even if shrouded in haze,
to know this hemped advance is worth risking
that its knotted hook has firmly latched
round rock solid as Uluru, wide and earth-caught as Ben Bulben
and not some sycamore half-rotted in its core
that taking my weight on crossing will loosen
shake its soil to moaning winds, wrenching, uprooting
plummet me mute
leaden and wingless
to the pit.

Australia
September 1983

AFTER CARRINGBUSH CEILI

for Brendan and John

This dark is sensuous
that spreads its palms across the day
fingering away light needed for shadows
embering these candles in the mirror's glaze.
Paul's house in Tinning Street
finds us collected in an odd assortment of
humour and pain,
gorged upon the sounds of Ireland.

The fiddle is stilled
but the fiddler strung tight
will not, cannot terminate
jig and swirl and loop
of inner dance,
recites to us his turnstile memories
the twirl and cut of paths to his regret.

You convince, Brendan,
there is still an appetite for the wandering exile
who plays relentless tunes of tugging hope,
spinning in fragments before the eye
that shadowed cool of the Clare Glens,
each crevice of the Burren.
Frenetic place-seeker
figure flickering now with the flames' reflection,
whose fervour cannot rest
whose drama is himself.

What is it that breathes swift and quiet
on the back of your neck, curling to shiver
driving you on —
yourself, your reflection perhaps
or that potent mix of bloodied cross and mother-need?

The banjo is stilled
but this player sits steady
Claddagh ring glimmering gold.
No agitation baulks you John
though the trill ripples you
and within, the landscape of tunes dips and turns,
your mind recurring rhythm.
No need for words here,
though later in the silence of others' sleep
your smile deepens
talk tumbles into laughter,
some sweet understanding,
and the comfort of touch in soothing darkness
soft as the flutter of fingers on strings
the light, treble-bright fluidity of your
warm and guileless heart.

Here is a way loneliness is put aside
              momentarily;
to become part of this night, its candle-lit camaraderie,
to be brim-full of music, saturated through heart and

mind and flesh, so there is no room for thought
stamped under dancing feet, smacked aside briefly
in some far corner of the empty hall;
to find one who will listen to our story
close their arms tight round us
till dawn files off the night and finds us
stronger for the telling.

SURVIVING SINGLE

for Lynne, Dale, Renate

I lie in sluggishly, relishing noise and smell.
Rain thrapples the iron roof,
a waft of fresh coffee insinuates up the stairs,
voices rise with it laughing and croissant-light.
Few sounds are sweeter
than the voices of women in early morning
building themselves toward the day.
Friendship purrs vibrant through these rooms.

Tomorrow waits tedious —
your fuse and split of
voices will be gone,
a cough, a fever
weighting me to bed
in the drab procession of illness.

Loneliness throws its shawl of rents across the days.
Too many pegs, too few clothes
twist along the empty line.
I panic when some interruption jolts my ritual of
dinner in synchrony with radio news,
as if a companion had suddenly left the table
leaving me to eat alone and foolish.
Pain furrows the hollow steadiness of my voice
when I say I am alright,
floods my eyes unexpectedly in the street
and frightened, I sandbag for control.

I hold myself now a moment
within the gold cocoon of your loving
knowing the silence to come
the long playing out of life;
knowing from a childhood lived in the sea
there's one way only to reach shore
when the tide turns crazy —
swim with the rip . . .

Australia
November 1983

OFFERINGS

for A

These rags of language
friends wrap round our wounds
they continue to tear in strips
from their own lives
seeking to comfort.

These are the remnants of beauty
people still carry with them
after the rush, the smog, the children, their weariness
have taken most of their searching from them;
after their need has ceased to tug at them
to stretch body and mind toward that life-jet
flooding them with pleasure, piercing pain,
the lovely, endless, tortuous climbing of that summitless peak.
Drained, they still have this giving left to bind with.

That moment at Dun Laoghaire
I watched and listened
crouched small
in a tight corner
of boats and tackle
while sea slushed and swashed
against the jetty
rocking to and fro on pylons,
the dark comfort of water
thudding deep beneath;

weeping for me, for you
for the great sadness of Paul
who lay bare and dying
at thirty-two
while they made drugged promises
death would not keep.

Your note says he is dead now,
that emptiness crowds you.
I hold to the memory of my stumble from the jetty
along the rubble and mud of railway backtracks, toward
you, crazy to live after your first close-up
contact with the death to come,
finding in the debris, alien as a flute in desert wind,
the lilac bloom of buddleia
one full-headed spray of blossom we carried back
savouring its subtle fragrance —
you told me even earnest bees cannot penetrate its sweetness
only butterflies with their tempered casual flit of wing.

These rags I hold out to you,
my tattered words,
all I have to offer —
these, and that lilac bloom
caught fresh in the mind
as when first-picked.

REASSESSING

Living alone now
sounds of a house are relearned.
It bends, creaks, stretches, familiarizing itself
to one, not two,
grinding a different tempo to my life
worn together, we shuffle, snuggle, me coned inside its
shelter.

This bird too
constantly chattering amid the spiked nudity
of that over-pruned apple tree, once sun-block to the kitchen,
I had noticed
only as accustomed backdrop seasounds
not as sparrow; audacious grey-brown character of some
substance.

It will perch
eventually against the window pecking
periodic incessant tapnotes on the glass, my house, this shell.
I had thought
there must be some horde of bird-
appetite-delights invisible to mere human taste

which lingered on
the pane beyond rain's wash,
sun's blaze, the scraping file-sharp tongue of wind.

But now I fancy
astonished as if gazing on fields green-crisped
drawn pure after clouded skies burst hard across their
                                                    dustiness

it is communication:

intention to break through

DOLPHINS

Tonight's play *Dolphins* is too apt.
Clarity and doubt blur among
squeak voices
eerie in the theatre's cavernous echo
their tone querying,
messages hanging in code

Travelling dark back roads home
between the salty silent twist of misted gums
my mind fills with gurgle and whistle,
dolphins screeching entrapment
their pools bland, secure.
And just over the wall
air white with it,
rush of whirling surf
tongues sensuous between the rocks

Liberators face unenviable choice:
to break open the gates
risking the dolphins
innocent, untried, vulnerable
in the wild dangerous treachery of a sea
full of hunters and blue surprise;
or leave them safe to cosseted old age
their quality of bemusement intact
comforted by the known
swimming round tight circular boundaries
of the tank into
curvature of the spine

if

and if i were god i would so love the world i would
not give outside my right the son some woman's body
        bled into life

i would take their crosses from those who suffer in ways
profuse as stars in milky clarity of summer nights
        snatch their wooden torment

smash match small leaving only agony of growth
suffering of self bandaged in old scrawny comfort love
        for what other reason be god?

BLACK SPRING

I pause in London to catch breath
anticipation's charm
blinding me to omens.
Black ice of winter is shattered
but sunlight seems lost
in corridors of smirched brick.
Shards of growth splinter
breaking the green,
daffodils spike sharp.
Wind turns its bezel edge to my face
catches in gutters.
Spring comes harsh this year and late
forcing a rough ache in the branch
a slowing throb in the pursed lips of buds.
Flesh too, over-ripe
after the long holding back,
weeps for touch.

But in Ireland
winter has yielded.
I watch its opening thighs
release the anguish of growth
the million times over promise of
colour and scent and soft fluttering life.
Bluebells bright and the
canary gaiety of gorse and dandelion
are flung into the glens' floss of green.
Cherry blossom snows pink and fresh
into lanes and ditches,
hawthorn whiskers whiten the hedgerow.

Heat thawing life
breaks to vulnerable translucence
the beech and larch leaves
that this week will harden dark.

Tricks of the mind
blend beginnings and endings into confusion,
we slip too easily into familiar patterns
of covert loving.
This time we will climb our mountain casually to picnic
simply sharing brown bread, beer and cheese
doing the things that lovers do
in the saffron promise of spring,
without caress

and it will not work.

The willow we plant for bees,
sapling sure,
waves its tentacled dance through breezed tomorrow
readying itself to last
far beyond the passing of our small time.
And you await the new queen
constantly clearing the hives
of potential challenge,
ruthlessly digging out
their white mucus beginnings,
unaware that her future will be stung to death.
Side by side in summer past
we have spun the honey,

watched those frames fling up their load
drenched in its amber sweat.
Breathless over the spinning drum
wringing out sweetness
arm-hairs are dropletted
skin licked with it
hair smells of it.
Simplicity is one way:
a bee travels
twice round the world
for a pound of honey.
Such time, such energy
                such patience,
such small return.

I envy you. Self-contained, invulnerable,
you are sealed now.
But for me
to flow
be *in* things
drowned
smothered
of the honey itself
is the only entrance,
the only path.

It does not work.
We cannot make over into casual warmth
zest that fed a leaping furnace.
The future must forget

your summer skin;
that strangely confident gait
treading down boyhood rejection;
the Kerry-blue of your eyes
their seasons of doubt and burning.
Life will proceed now with a
pointless accuracy.
Strange that we have lived this time
with it all still tangled inside.
Who spared me
that long grey drag of winter,
for this thaw wasted
withering under a black sun?

Ireland
May 1st 1984
A

MURROE

Grey heron I have seen elsewhere
lifts untrusting from the Mulcair in late evening
before blaze of darkness inks its flight invisible.
Sun's displaced Aegean clarity has bounced from earth
its absence burnishing sky to pewter blue,
warmth oozing from grey stone bridge
into my belly soothing
I press into it for carnal comfort leaning after the bird
whose flight had so broken still afterlight.
The bevel of river angles haphazard between rocks
slushing sounds like a soul wading towards me
perhaps the bird mistook too.
Everyone is tidying up relics of past seasons
tying the dead ends of winter.
Fires far off burn gathered debris.

Night will come in on me so swiftly I will not hear its tread
but that swift surge of regret flushing body will note it
one last time before sleep

AHEAD

a rookless sky awaits
and no amount of dreaming
can call them from the crag's unbroken peace

Mithimna, Lesvos
July 1984
A

RECURRENT TUG

Tempted by the dazzling fly
tweezered to glimmer green and gold in sunslant
I swallowed.
No feast.
Only delicate silver precision of
hook
sliding from throat to gut.
Pain grows its own familiar comfort,
between the tug and pull of waves,
slack masquerades as freedom.
What will it take
shorter and less wearying
than waiting for rot, decay,
to urge me, strengthen me
for the wrench to rip-twist free?

Bloodied beyond repair
half alive
scarred with loss
slashed through with regret
I struggle with the hook.

And your shade made flesh
still walks in trespass
the land of the living,
green sanctuary
so far, so far
from this beaten ancient scorch.
But pagan similitude
links temple to church

touch memories are caught.
White and lavender herbs
flower wildly among cypress and rock,
crushed between thumb and finger
their scent fuels hunger.

Tears fall
shell-sheen beneath the moon.
Her path glints many-eyed on waves
toward the cliff
each lid silvered for seduction.
Dark is wet with grief
night's pierced pupil floods sky with it,
reason drowns in yearning.
Only flesh and memory live.
Desire flames in breast and thigh.
In groves, gnarled trees are shaken, shaken
till the olives fall.
What harvest is this?

PART FIVE

Ireland
December 1984
A

WINTER SURFACES

Rain varnished the leaves
and has vanished.
Sun gleam cuts
into frosted trees.
Atop the Cliffs of Moher
throwing ourselves against
the icy blast
we flatten our bodies
on slush and mud
to hang our heads
over crumbling edges
stretching towards the fall.
Below, beyond the clawing sea
Aran Islands are anchored
in a day smothered in blue.

How odd we are.
The Abbey waits
frosting over;
we eat, drink and talk,
like ordinary people.
We are not.
We skim iced surfaces
professional skaters now,
keeping our fantasies closed
sharing what we can.

At Millbank House
I sit by blazing turf
waiting to leave again:

brown bread, honey and tea,
the ritual of the photographs
where the children grow.
Miss O'Neill wept
when I gave her freesias.
Frail at seventy-two
I ache that she'll remain
to pull my guinness again and reminisce.
The Mulcair gushes full
beside the long walk to Declan's house
still not lived in.

These things regulate the year
in another life.
It *is* worth the struggle
to keep of this what is warm and glowing,
not to lose all
because having all is impossible;
to remake a different frame
a different name.
And what is impossible
must be learned.

Ireland
January 1985
A

THE FINAL SEASON

You always thought
action is in the speaking of it.
But speech is not the act.

The grey-white of snow skies,
the light-bloom of cold
into which these bare trees spread
free of leaf and
summer's torn glaze,
are those where my heron
had sought its peace.

I always thought summer the loving season,
but was wrong.
Look how naked winter makes us.

Now we join in releasing barbs
worn one-by-one through strength.
Slim steel dissolves, compulsion's scars heal.
But parting we draw close
as cold hands about a guttering flame.
Then touch
fires the ebbing passion.

Rose-coloured loving —
curtain, sheet, lamplight,
the inner fragile flush of shells.

Blue eyes desire, confused.
Lines of your aging mirror mine.

I memorise
your feathery brow beneath my thumb,
each changing moment of this long last breath,
withholding endearment
the time long past.

Your breath will linger in my hair;
silk of me beneath you will wake you nights
hands searching the sheets, somnambulist in loving.

Bonds of ambivalence, the knowledge of endings.
Almost too late in this season between rain and sleet,
night has given us yesterday's promise.
We move toward something
we can neither touch nor keep.
And now, at last, I know that all my passion
cannot make sure your green will live.

I let go the last hook,
knowing you will remember flesh in flesh,
ache, now and then, for summers and springs;

for nights that were star-swollen over black turf,
bog cotton whimpering under whispering trees;
for those mountain climbs that fed
the flare of pain and struggle we burned
to feel we were alive:
for all we relished in the joy
and anguished raging of our hearts.

Ireland
July 1987
A

SPENT

No honey this summer,
few flowers and the bees have gone slumbering.
Iris-blue skies but no warmth, and
rhododendrons that exploded pink and purple
in the spring,
brown into yesterday.

So moments leave us.

On the Cliffs of Moher, seabirds circle screaming,
wind whips the ocean to rainbow froth
spirals up, clinging,
a kind of damp confetti.
Grounded, our wet clothes flap
unable to fly.

We weigh like lead.

You flame burning against the sun, and
we come full circle: you alight, fierce, and
I, whole, resisting, as we first met.
Now you whisper you want me.
Now you cannot hold back.
Eyes flood blue with tears.

Now is too late.

You try.
You call me back
in the many ways
a lover knows,
learned from the years
when my need split open, derelict.

Tricks learned to hobble a heart.

Years of stolen time:
a broken prism, spectrum released
bold and untouchable,
countless fires of the darkest opal
flashing ever-elusive
in the twist of stone.

Spilling between us, memories sweet with longing.

Then I was feverish with living
caught in love's endless giving,
my fraying heart frantic
to keep you green and growing,
a frenzied rosella scattering its
rainbow-sparkler afterlight.

Scratches of colour only, in the gathering gloom.

So sure I could give you my full bright world,
I made love gallop riderless toward the darkening lake.
I fought the world's black knights;
fear, uncertainty, custom, the rules of god and man.
Too much, too much
there was too much passion there in that wild place.

I am dead with it.

We cannot love now
and remake the past.
I will live only in the present
no longer breaking
on the bluff's upturned claws
in waves of pain.

I am not bruising to know I'm alive.

And I know the hook,
its fiery gleam
slipped behind the moment.
Neither wind nor gull knows
the tempest let loose by longing
and me, the twisting kite played out along its current.

These hands tore the hook out.

Only a fool would welcome
that salt, that pain, a second time.
I am the rock on which the sea now breaks
desire hardened across years, oceans,
pulling, pushing me, as if it fed you to know
I could not escape loving you.

I no longer value games of risk.

Later by the river in the glen,
you splay on rocks
a lizard soaking in sun
not quite sure of what is lost
as heat leaves the afternoon.
You pick a rose, 'for us, for memory'.

Bowerbirds, we go on hoarding.

THE STORM

*'so you refuse and then you discover that your house is haunted by
the ghost of a leopard.'*

Jeanette Winterson *The Passion*

I dream of your desire
shock awake to it
throbbing in the air
in the white fire
scorching the sky.
So fierce —
a lather of light to write by.
Thunder of your need
rockets over the night,
beats up winds to
pummel the silky oak,
throws off wanton rain, in a
shaggy shaking from the hidden den.

I feel you here
so far across the oceans
your scent is buried in my sleep.
I rise naked in the dark tremble.
You blaze behind me
warm palms on shoulders
sweet breath at the nape.
Turning me, you take my cool wrist
laying it against your burning cheek
sliding your tongue up long inside my arm:
'choose; let me love you'.

You should not have come so far
on such a night.
You should not have called all this up
dynamitic and raging.
Passion is spent,
thrill of it no longer seduces.

And yet, you tempt,
still.
Your night-wild yearning
stirs the pink softness of fig flesh
to fragile betrayal.

Anyway,
it's only a storm.

TO SATISFY

Scent of mock orange caught in breezes
once should be enough,
bolled bright wattle glimpsed through tangle-leaf
once should be enough,
held *once* the rush of him full
as high tide floods this cave

     should be enough.

These will not last:
tide will ebb
blossom fade and fracture
spring sweetness

     fold against burnt summer.

       But

       we

above all reason season or creatures run wild with it
    crave permanence

our films must never flicker to blank screen,
houses not crumble, grey rock to ivy,
lives enter newness when flesh frays to freckled death,
    we call it God.

And our loves
must prove as nothing else can
        eternity.

Yet they are all
one flash flare of short fuse flame
        searing across the eye.

A breath in quick, a zoom pulse *once*
        should be enough.

GLOSSARY OF NAMES AND WORDS

Glenstal Abbey — *Glenstal* (*pron.* glen-stall) is the English version of 'Gleann stail', meaning 'glen of the stallion'. The Glen is rich in wildflowers, and the Abbey is surrounded by forests of rhododendron and honeysuckle. There are five lakes in the grounds, and a wildlife sanctuary. Built in 1839 to look like a twelfth-century castle with a gatehouse and round tower, it was owned privately until it came into the hands of the church in 1926. It is now a Benedictine monastery, a private boys school, a farm, and wildlife sanctuary.

Ben Bulben — a large solid outcrop of rock near Sligo.

The Burren (*pron.* burrn) — a rocky limestone area in County Clare, 40 kilometres long by 24 kilometres wide. For so barren a place, the Burren has an astonishing array of wildflowers, many of them rare specimens, and is never out of bloom. In the eastern Burren is Coole Park, near the town of Gort, where Lady Gregory gathered the literati of her day. Nearby was Yeats' summer house Thoor Ballylee, where he wrote *The Tower* and *The Winding Stair*.

The Claddagh (*pron.* clada) — a ring of claddagh design, which has two hands clasping a heart surmounted by a crown. Of medieval origin (1690), it became closely associated with the fishing town of Claddagh near Galway. Used as a betrothal or wedding ring or as a ring of love, it symbolises friendship, love and loyalty.

Cliffs of Moher (*pron.* mower) — majestic cliffs in County Clare, 8 kilometres in length and rising 200 metres from the Atlantic.

Galtée Móre (*pron.* gal-tea more) — the third highest mountain in Ireland, situated at the beautiful Glen of Aherlow (*pron.* a-her-low, a as in cat).

Innisfree (*pron.* innish-free) — an island in Lough Gill near Sligo about which Yeats wrote his famous poem 'The Lake Isle of Innisfree'.

Uluru (*pron.* oo-loo-roo) — the Aboriginal name for Ayers Rock, a large outcrop of rock in central Australia.

OTHER BOOKS AVAILABLE FROM SPINIFEX PRESS

ANGELS OF POWER
AND OTHER REPRODUCTIVE CREATIONS
edited by Susan Hawthorne and Renate Klein

1991 Australian Feminist Book Fortnight Favourite

In the tradition of Mary Shelley's *Frankenstein*, the writers in this book use technological developments as their starting point in tracing the consequences of reproductive technologies. Imagination, vision and humour come together and demonstrate that women can resist the power of godlike scientists who long to create monsters and angels. With contributions by writers from Australia, New Zealand, Canada and USA.

'*Angels of Power* is an important ground-breaking anthology ...' – Karen Lamb, *Age*.

'*Angels of Power* should head the reading list of any course in ethics and reproductive technology.' – Karin Lines, *Editions*.

'... renders ethical issues imaginatively through fiction and contributes significantly to this important debate.' – Irina Dunn, *Sydney Morning Herald*.

SYBIL: THE GLIDE OF HER TONGUE
by Gillian Hanscombe

'Gillian Hanscombe performs a feat of lesbian imagination in this stunning sequence. Her sybilic voice, familiar and strange at once, radiates both vision and anger in a prose that echoes the music of our thoughts back to us. *Sybil* gives us a lesbian erotic, a lesbian politics, a lesbian tradition, grounded in what Suniti Namjoshi defines as the prophetic. Welcome to lesbian imagination singing at full range.'

– Daphne Marlatt

'That *Sybil* happily bears comparison with the works of Sappho, Virginia Woolf and Adrienne Rich is, in my view, a measure of just how important this work is to lesbian literature, and therefore to literature in general.'

– Suniti Namjoshi

'*Sybil: The Glide of Her Tongue* is a prophetic fugue in lesbian past, present and future time, Sybilline tidings of lesbian existence.' – Mary Meigs

'O I am enamoured of *Sybil*. Gillian Hanscombe is one of the most insightfully ironic, deliciously lyrical voices we have writing amongst us today.' – Betsy Warland

'A book where the lesbian voice meditates the essential vitality of she dykes who have visions. A book where Gillian Hanscombe's poetry opens up meaning in such a way that it provides for beauty and awareness, for a space where one says yes to a lesbian we of awareness.' – Nicole Brossard

'*Sybil* is an exciting and compelling work. It is hard to think of any poet in Australia who can equal Hanscombe's virtuosity and power.'

– Bev Roberts, *Australian Book Review.*

THE FALLING WOMAN
by Susan Hawthorne

Top Twenty Title, New Zealand Women's Book Festival, 1992

The Falling Woman memorably dramatises a desert journey in which two women confront ancient and modern myths, ranging from the Garden of Eden to the mystique of epilepsy, and the mysteries of the universe itself. In the guise of three personae – Stella, Estella, Estelle – the falling woman struggles to find the map for her life and meet the challenge of her own survival.

'A remarkable, lyrical first novel that weaves together such disparate themes as the mystery of epilepsy, love between women, and an odyssey across the Australian desert.' – *Ms Magazine*.

'Hawthorne shows assurance, a powerful historical and cultural imagination and a rich feel for language.' – John Hanrahan, *Age*.

'This is a beautiful book, written with powerful insight and captivating originality.' – Julia Hancock, *LOTL*.

IF PASSION WERE A FLOWER
Lariane Fonseca

'Here the shadows of the plants were miraculously distinct. She noticed the separate grains of earth in the flower beds as if she had a microscope stuck to her eye. She saw the intricacy of the twigs of every tree. Each blade of grass was distinct and the markings of the veins and petals.'

— Virginia Woolf, *Orlando.*

If Passion Were a Flower – Inspired by the writing of Virginia Woolf and the paintings of Georgia O'Keefe, Lariane Fonseca's photographs make us look again at the flowers around, and begin anew to appreciate their beauty and sensuality.

Lariane Fonseca was born in Bombay and now lives in Geelong, Australia where she holds exhibitions and co-runs a women's bookshop.

RU 486:
MISCONCEPTIONS, MYTHS AND MORALS
Renate Klein, Janice G. Raymond and Lynette J. Dumble

Human Rights Award, Certificate of Commendation (Non-fiction) 1991

A controversial book about the new French abortion pill. The authors examine the medical literature on the drug, including its adverse effects. They evaluate the social, medical and ethical implications, including the use of women for experimental research, in particular third world populations, and the importance of women-controlled abortion clinics. The book is excellent case study material for medical, health and women's studies practitioners and students.

The authors are experts in feminist ethics, women's health and medical science.

'This book makes an important contribution to the debate surrounding RU 486, a debate which the tragedies of history – those associated with other reprodutive technologies – tell us, we have every need to involve ourselves in, to acquaint ourselves with and above all, to have our say in. *RU 486 ...* [is] unique even in feminist scholarship.'
– Kim Webster, *Australian Women's Book Review.*

'*RU 486: Misconceptions, Myths and Morals* is an important contribution to a discussion which until recently has been dominated by drug company press releases ... I consider this book of great value to pro-choice/abortion activists.'
– Claudine Holt, *Green Left.*